Sunny Day

Edited by Gillian Doherty

First published in 2008 by Usborne Publishing Ltd, 83-85 Saffron Hill, London EC1N 8RT, England.
www.usborne.com Copyright © 2008 Usborne Publishing Ltd.
The name Usborne and the devices are Trade Marks of Usborne Publishing Ltd. All rights reserved.
No part of this publication may be reproduced, stored in a retrieval system, or transmitted in any form or
by any means, electronic, mechanical, photocopying, recording or otherwise, without the prior permission
of the publisher. First published in America in 2008. UE. Printed in Dubai.

Sunny Day

Anna Milbourne

Illustrated by Elena Temporin

Designed by Laura Parker

Early in the morning, the sun peeps over the edge of the world...

...and floods everything with light.

Have you ever wondered
why some days are sunny
and some are not?

It's because sometimes
the sun is hidden by clouds.

But if the clouds drift away,
it becomes a sunny day.

On a sunny day, sunflowers
turn to face the sun.

They look as if they're watching
as it creeps across the sky.

A butterfly spreads her pretty wings and basks in the sunshine.

When she's warm enough to fly...

...she flutter-flutter-flits away.

Sunshine makes flowers open their petals.

Busy bees buzz around...

buzzzzzzzz

buzzzzzzz

buzzzzzzz

...sucking sweet juice called nectar
from the middle of each flower.

The bees hurry back to their hive...

...and give the nectar to the bees inside...

...who store it carefully
in funny-shaped holes.

Slowly it will turn into
delicious, golden honey.

By noon, the sun
is high in the sky.

There's shelter from its heat...

...in the cool shadows
under the cherry tree.

The sun's hot rays help
cherries grow juicy and sweet.

Noisy crickets chirrup
in the long, dry grass.

They're rubbing their wings
to make a creaky tune...

hoping other crickets
will want to meet them.

chirrup
chirrup

The sun sinks through the afternoon,
and mellows to a yellow haze.

Baby swallows are learning to fly.

Their parents swoop across the sky.

Gracefully they dip and dive,
catching teeny-tiny flies.

Later, when the sun is low...

shadows grow ver-r-r-y

ver-r-r-r-r-r-y long.

At the end of the day, the sun goes down
and bathes the sky in a rosy glow.

Let's hope tomorrow
is another sunny day.